Music Minus One Vocals

SING

CHRISTMAS SONGS

2139

CONTENTS

ISBN 978-1-941566-39-8

MMO 2139

We Wish You A Merry Christmas

Traditional
English carol

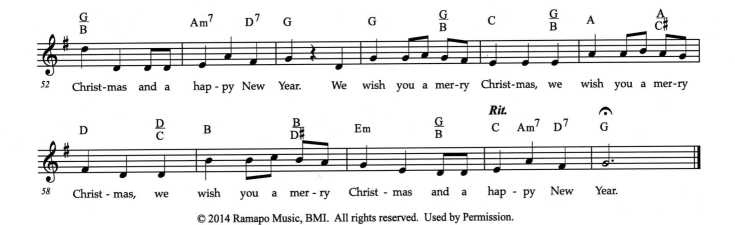

Christ-mas and a hap-py New Year. We wish you a mer-ry Christ-mas, we wish you a mer-ry

Christ-mas, we wish you a mer-ry Christ-mas and a hap-py New Year.

Angels We Have Heard On High

Traditional
French carol

An-gels we have heard on high sweet-ly sing-ing o'er the plains,

and the moun-tains in re-ply ech-o-ing their joy-ous strains. Glo

- ri - a in ex-cel-sis De - o, Glo

- ri - a in ex-cel-sis De - o.

Shep-herds, why this jub-i-lee? Why your joy-ous strains pro-long?

6

Frosty The Snowman

Steve Nelson
and Jack Robbins

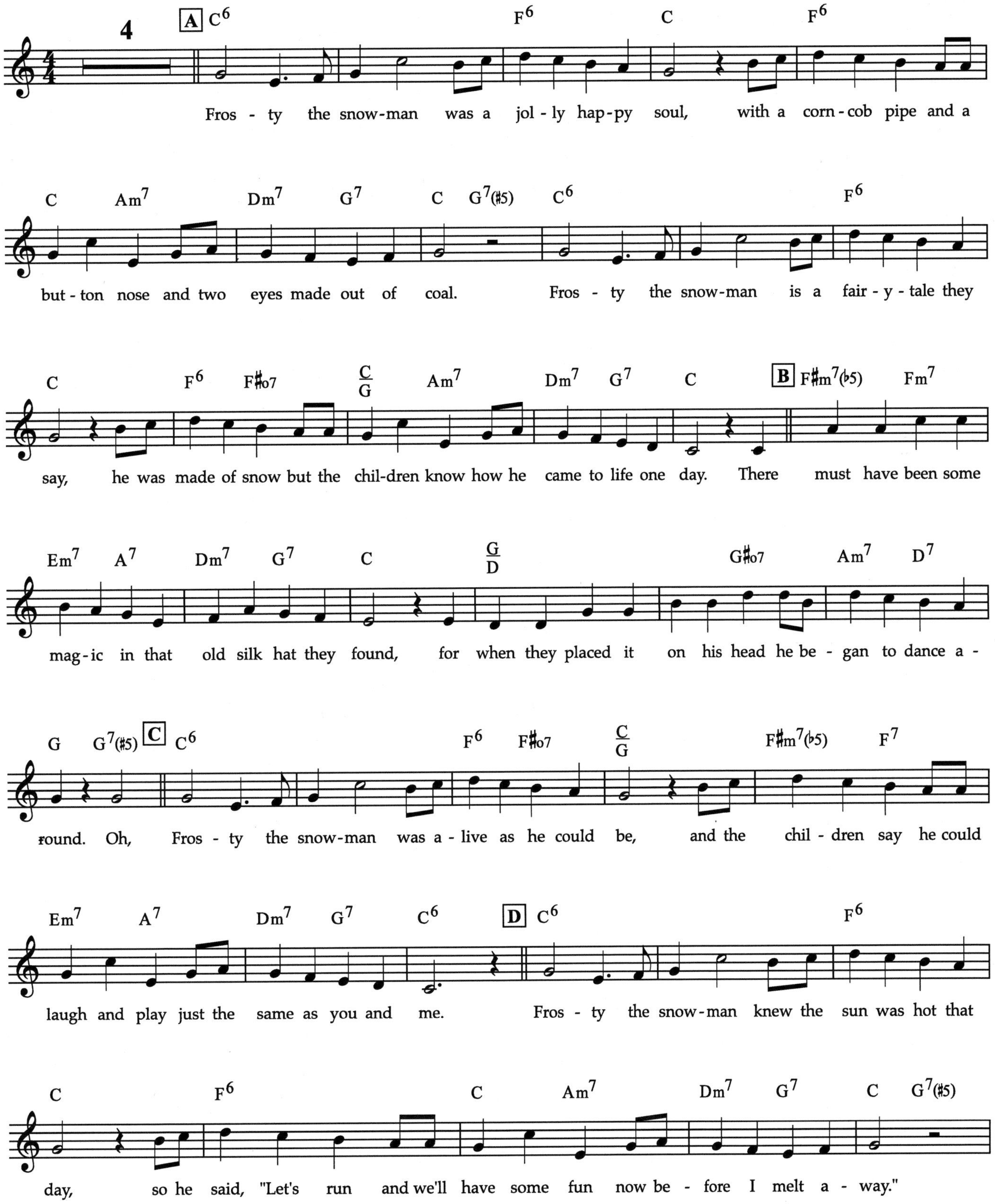

8

Down to the vil-lage with a broom-stick in his hand run-ning here and there all a-round the square say-ing

"Catch me if you can." He led them down the streets of town right to that traf-fic

cop, and he on-ly paused a mo-ment when he heard him hol-ler "Stop!" for

Fros-ty the snow-man had to hur-ry on his way but he waved good-by say-ing, "Don't you cry, I'll be

back a-gain some day." Thump-i-ty thump thump, thumpi-ty thump thump, look at Fros-ty

go. Thump-i-ty thump thump, thumpi-ty thump thump, o-ver the hills of snow.

Feliz Navidad

Jose Feliciano

Fe-liz Na-vi - dad, Fe-liz Na-vi - dad, Fe-liz Na-vi-

-dad, pros - per-o a - ño y fel-i-ci-dad. Fe-liz Na-vi - dad,

9

Fe-liz Na-vi - dad, Fe-liz Na-vi - dad, pros - per-o a - ño y fel-i - ci-dad.

I wan-na wish you a mer-ry Christmas, I wan-na wish you a mer-ry Christ-mas,

I wan-na wish you a mer - ry Christ-mas from the bot-tom of my heart.

I wan-na wish you a mer-ry Christmas, I wan-na wish you a mer-ry Christ-mas, I wan-na wish you a

mer-ry Christmas from the bot-tom of my heart. Fe-liz Na-vi heart.

Copyright © J & H Publishing Corp. International Copyright Secured

Joy To The World

George F. Handel
and Isaac Watts

Joy to the world, the Lord is come. Let earth re-ceive her King. Let

ev' - ry heart pre-pare Him room, and heav'n and na-ture sing, and heav'n and na-ture sing, and

heav'n and heav'n - and na-ture sing. He rules the world with truth and grace and

10

makes the na - tions prove the glo - ries_ of_____ His right - eous - ness_____ and

won - ders of His love, and_ won - ders of His love, and_ won - ders won - ders of His love.

C Joy to the world, the Lord is come. Let earth re - ceive her King. Let

ev'_ ry_ heart_____ pre - pare_ Him_ room,_____ and heav'n and na - ture_ sing, and_

heav'n and na - ture_ sing, and_ heav'n_____ and heav'n_____ and na - ture sing.

While Shepherds Watched Their Flocks

George F. Handel
and Nahum Tate

While shep - herds watched their flocks by __ night all __ seat - ed on the __

ground, _ the _ an - gel of the Lord came _ down and _ glo - ry shown a - round, _ and

glo - ry shown a - round. "Fear _ not," he said, for migh - ty __ dread had __ seized their troub - led __

Pat-a-Pan

Bernard de la Monnoye

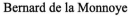

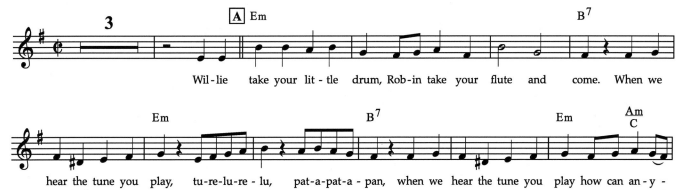

Deck The Halls

Traditional
Welsh carol

We Three Kings

John Henry Hopkins

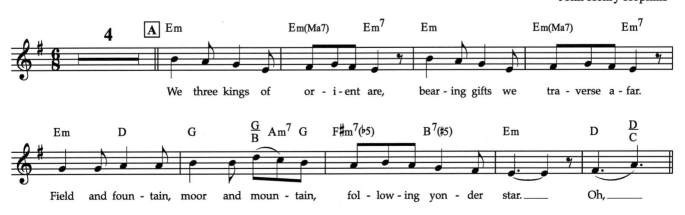

star of won-der, star of night, star with roy-al beau-ty bright, west-ward lead-ing, still pro-ceed-ing,

guide us to thy per-fect Light. Glor-ious now be-hold Him a-rise, King and God and

sa-cri-fice. Al-le-lu-ia, al-le-lu-ia, heav'n to Earth re-plies.___

Oh,___ star of won-der, star of night, star with roy-al beau-ty bright,

west-ward lead-ing, still pro-ceed-ing, guide us to thy per-fect Light.

Away In A Manger

James R. Murray

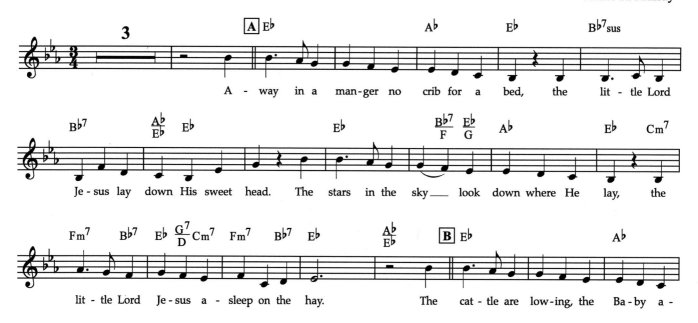

A-way in a man-ger no crib for a bed, the lit-tle Lord

Je-sus lay down His sweet head. The stars in the sky___ look down where He lay, the

lit-tle Lord Je-sus a-sleep on the hay. The cat-tle are low-ing, the Ba-by a-

(All I Want for Christmas is) My Two Front Teeth

Donald Y. Gardner

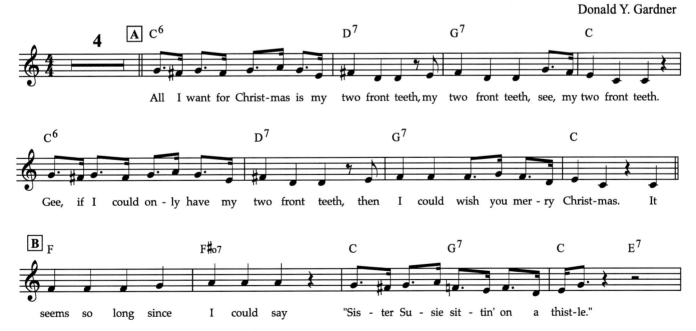

16

Over The River And Through The Woods

Lydia Maria Child

grand-ma's cap I spy, hoo-ray for fun, the pud-ding's done, hoo-ray for pump-kin pie.

D O-ver the riv-er and through the woods to grand-moth-er's house we go, the horse knows the way to

car-ry the sleigh through white and drift-ed snow. O-ver the riv-er and through the woods, oh

how the wind does blow, it stings the toes and bites the nose as o-ver the ground we

go. It stings the toes and bites the nose as o-ver the ground we go.

Jingle Bells

James Pierpont

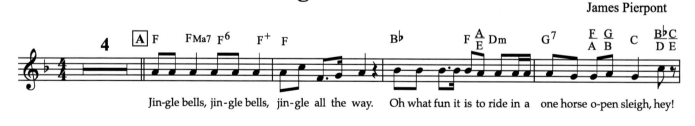

Jin-gle bells, jin-gle bells, jin-gle all the way. Oh what fun it is to ride in a one horse o-pen sleigh, hey!

Jin-gle bells, jin-gle bells, jin-gle all the way. Oh what fun it is to ride in a one horse o-pen sleigh.

Dash-ing through the snow in a one horse o-pen sleigh, o'er the fields we go, laugh-ing all the way.

Bells on bob-tails ring mak-ing spir-its bright, what fun it is to ride and sing a sleigh-ing song to-night Oh,

jin-gle bells, jin-gle bells, jin-gle all the way. Oh what fun it is to ride in a one horse o-pen sleigh, hey!

Jin-gle bells, jin-gle bells, jin-gle all the way. Oh what fun it is to ride in a one horse o-pen sleigh.

Jin-gle bells, jin-gle bells, jin-gle all the way. Oh what fun it is to ride in a one horse o-pen sleigh, hey!

Jin-gle bells, jin-gle bells, jin-gle all the way. Oh what fun it is to ride in a one horse o-pen sleigh.

Go Tell It On The Mountain

John Wesley Work Jr.

Go tell it on the moun - tain, o - ver the hills and e - v'ry - where.

20

Hark The Herald Angels Sing

Felix Mendelssohn
and William H. Cummings

Je - sus, — our Em - man - u - el. Hark, the her - ald an - gels sing, "Glo - ry — to the

new - born King" Hail the hea'vn - born Prince of Peace, — hail the Son of

Right - eous - ness. Light and life, to all He brings, — ris'n with heal - ing

in His wings. Mild He lays his glo - ry by, — born that men no

more may die, — born to raise the sons of Earth, born to — give them

sec - ond birth. Hark, the her - ald an - gels sing, "Glo - ry — to the new - born King."

Rudolph The Red-Nosed Reindeer

Johnny Marks

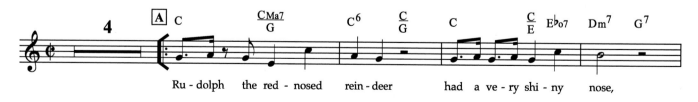

Ru - dolph the red - nosed rein - deer had a ve - ry shi - ny nose,

The First Noel

Traditional
English carol

24

Here We Come A-Caroling

Traditional
English carol

-wise the mis-tress too, and all the lit-tle chil-dren that round the ta-ble go. Love and

joy come to you, and to you glad Christ-mas too, and God bless you and send_ you a

hap-py New Year, and God send you a hap-py New Year._

O Come All Ye Faithful

John Francis Wade

Oh come all ye faith-ful, joy-ful and tri-

-um-phant, oh come ye, oh come_ ye to Beth-le-hem. Come and be-hold Him,

born the King of an-gels. Oh come let us a-dore Him, oh

come let us a-dore Him, oh come let us a-dore Him,_ Christ_ the Lord.

Silent Night

Franz Gruber

Good Christian Men Rejoice

Johann Sebastian Bach

Good Chris - tian men re - joice,____ with heart and soul and voice.____

Give ye heed to what we say, news, news, Je - sus Christ is born to-day. Ox and ass be -

-fore him bow, and He is in the man-ger now. Christ is born to - day,____ Christ is born to - day.

Good Chris - tian men re - joice,____ with heart and soul and voice.____

Now ye hear of end-less bliss, joy, joy, Je - sus Christ was born for this. He has o - pened

hea - ven's door, and man is bless-ed ev - er-more. Christ was born for this,____ Christ was born for

this. Good Chris-tian men re-joice,____ with heart and soul and voice.____ Now ye need not

fear the grave, peace, peace, Je - sus Christ was born to save. Calls you one and calls you all to

gain His ev - er - last-ing hall. Christ was born to save,___ Christ was born to save.

It Came Upon A Midnight Clear

Edmund Sears and
Richard Storrs Willis

It came u - pon___ a mid - night clear, that glor - ious

song___ of old,_____ from an - gels ben - ding near the earth to

touch their harps___ of gold._____ Peace on the earth,___ good will to men, from

heav'n's___ all gra - cious King._____ The world in sol - emn still - ness

lay to hear the an - gels sing._____ For lo, the

days — are hast - 'ning on by pro - phets seen — of old, _____ when

with the e - ver cir - cling years shall come the time — fore - told. _____ When

the new heav'n — and earth shall own, the Prince — of Peace — their King, _____ and

the whole world — give back the song which now the an - gels sing. _____

Santa Claus Is Coming To Town

J. Fred Coots

You bet-ter watch out, you bet-ter not cry, bet-ter not pout, I'm tel-lin' you why,

San-ta Claus is com-in' to town. He's mak-in' a list, and check-in' it twice, gon-na find out who's

naugh-ty and nice, San-ta Claus is com-in' to town. He sees you when you're sleep-ing, he

knows when you're a-wake, he knows if you've been bad or good, so be good for good-ness sake. Oh you

bet-ter watch out, you bet-ter not cry, bet-ter not pout, I'm tel-lin' you why, San-ta Claus is

com-in' to town. You com-in' to town.

Nuttin' For Christmas

Sid Tepper and
Roy C. Bennett

I broke my bat on John-ny's head, some-bo-dy snitched on me. I

hid a frog in sis-ter's bed, some-bo-dy snitched on me. I spilled some ink on Mom-my's rug,

I made Tom-my eat a bug, bought some gum with a pen-ny slug, some-bo-dy snitched on

me. Oh I'm get-tin' nut-tin' for Christ-mas, Mom-my and Dad-dy are mad,

Music Minus One
50 Executive Boulevard • Elmsford, New York 10523-1325
914-592-1188 • e-mail: info@musicminusone.com
www.musicminusone.com

MMO 2139

ISBN 978-1-941566-39-8